Helium Heart

CARLIN PIERCE

Copyright © 2012 Carlin Pierce

All rights reserved.

ISBN: 1548646385
ISBN-13: 978-1548646387

for you

CONTENTS

This is not your average poetry collection. There are no titles, for there are no chapters in life and love, as much as we may wish for them. There are mismatched margins, unexpected words, and gut-wrenching, heart-shattering attempts at expression. Here lies a story of love and recovery in all its honest, infamous glory.

ACKNOWLEDGMENTS

To all those who gave me inspiration for these poems, thank you. To all those who knocked me down, thank you. To all those who helped me up, thank you. To all my lost girls; you are so strong, thank you.

*I didn't actually meet him the day I met him. He didn't speak to me
in any way other than presence that first day.*

She could have flown
   anytime she wanted.
      He knew, on some level,
   her helium heart.
   But she'd tied herself
      to his wrist
   to hover between him
      and the clouds.
   Because she knew that
   if she flew away,
      she'd know no gravity;
   she'd break
      trying to outrun the stars.

I sat beside him, and caught his eye once. For such a large man, his eyes were strangely disquieted. And in a moment I knew I had no chance of redemption.

Everything about you
hurts inside me
don't look at me
your eyes are too warm
and dark
I'm going to drown
when they melt my ice-cold heart.

Kiss me one last time
I can't unmake my memories.
I might as well,
drown in you by choice
if I'm going down with the ship
anyway.

HELIUM HEART

In the moment I didn't meet him, I realized I was fucked. So I stepped off that cliff willingly.

Falling, even at the best of times
        is terrifying
        because you know
        that sooner or later
        that the ground is falling up.
        And reality rarely
        strikes
        without leaving some bruises
    at the very least.

You have two choices. Either you give in to the darkness—revel in it and become
　　　just another specter that haunts this house. Or you become the light and vanquish all the
　　　　shadows.

"How do I become the light?"

Well for that you must set yourself on fire.

HELIUM HEART

I hoped when the fall stopped, when the adrenaline wore out, that the bottom would be an ocean, a sea to spare me shattering and that promised a horizon, eternal.

He was one of those people
you know you want in your life
until forever means nothing
anymore
and she knew that the moment she met him.

CARLIN PIERCE

He wishes now he'd picked her
    a wildflower
        she was
            but she deserved
                so much more
                    than to die by his hands,
                        pressed flat and preserved;
                  she deserved to die
            in a wildfire
        ravaged in her prime
      scorched to dust.
For beauty that luscious
should end how it existed:
    wild and perfect
where it breathed.

HELIUM HEART

I didn't know, and looking back I know I'd step anyway.

Maybe one day,
he'll realize
her eyes were the ones
he wanted to see
forever.

CARLIN PIERCE

    Shatter me with your whispers
of a magic I can only know
    if I open my heart.
Take my breath away
    I don't need it—
        I survive in your gentle laughter.
Feed me with your flaws
I love you for being human
I lie with the human in you,
    though I've a growing suspicion
        you're more god than man,
    and you chose me to be your angel.
        Don't hate me for the human
           in *my* hands.

HELIUM HEART

Holding onto someone who won't hold you back only makes the ocean freeze, but I still held, I hold, onto the hope that the ice is not glacial, that I can crack it when I hit head first (I flipped over in midair to a swan dive).

Sometimes *I love you* isn't good enough,
sometimes it's a cover up,
sometimes it means fuck off actually, because I don't want
                to address the problem.

We form connections to make our lives less empty,
less insignificant
and yet we are in constant conflict because
despite being classified, by ourselves no less, as social
                creatures,
we exist best alone.

When there is one person's back to watch, he does not
                sacrifice—
sacrifice entails "for a greater good"
a greater good implies a multiplicity
no virgins for the man who walks alone
no family for he who doesn't share footsteps.

Love though, that's the question …
To hell with existential crises
Hamlet was fucked anyway—
love, to love, to be in love, to attach
that's a dangerous undertaking

      because when verbalization is the only way to know
      when the one side becomes an enemy as much as friend

when *I love you* is what Hitler says
and sorry seems to be the hardest word…

What if we weren't meant to mate for life?
We are animals after all
animals don't mate for life
except ducks
        ducks mate for life.

HELIUM HEART

I met him truly, days after we started to quietly share the same space.
I learned his name, and he learned mine.

    He told me he didn't wear a watch.
    I knew that, I knew too much about him,
        he knew that too, I think.
    But the depth of his relationships
        were measured in the
            comfort of his silences.
                The watch, you see, shackled him
                    to life—reminded him
                      of his humanity,
                        inescapable.
                    Maybe that, that was why
                    he looked so sad—
            he's looking right
        through you,
      maybe he can see the future
  and he doesn't want to know
    how close it is.
      Yes, that would make sense, he, a seer;
      he could certainly see right through me.

CARLIN PIERCE

He didn't speak much, but I found, somehow, I didn't need him to.

>I like watching him
>when he does the thing he loves,
>when he feeds his soul
>it brings out his eyes,
>it pulls back the blinds,
>and in those open windows
candles burn.

Learn from these windows,
darling,
there's quite a soul
behind them.

write me softly
    off your tongue
truss me up
    in your lips
as you struggle to put
    me to words

HELIUM HEART

I also found myself craving him in the moments he wasn't with me—in the small of the night when my horrors came to haunt me.

He was her gentle giant,
her trampoline, her
umbrella in a
November storm,
and he'd never
know how much his presence
meant to a girl
who raised herself
on straw and sand.

CARLIN PIERCE

Somehow, he was warm enough to melt the rigid walls and wire I'd put up inside my head to compartmentalize my memories.

He tried to fix her—
she only loved something if it was broken.
And he, whole, could not draw her
    (a picture of the world
        compellingly shattered enough)
    to him, she was cracked glass
a little glue caressed onto her surface
    would seal her cracks
        to her, he was marble
            capable of being carved, only
            too strong to need fixing
            to love him she'd need to break him first.

HELIUM HEART

black heart
    cold hands
    tired eyes
    dead soul

"but smile, darling,
the world need you whole"

CARLIN PIERCE

Somehow, without trying, he came to be my white knight to protect me from everything I didn't want to face, from everything he understood I couldn't face. He protected me from myself.

"I don't know why I have
this stupid impulse
   to protect her.
She is an army unto herself,
an avalanche, a tsunami.
   She'll crush you
     if you prostrate before her.
I still feel the need
to throw myself
   in front of the world
     before it touches her.
But she's a warrior
you can see it in her eyes,
   you can hear it in her voice
     you can feel it in her thunder.
I'd still take all her obstacles
out of her path
   and though I know she'd sooner
     kill me for it-
       I'd still give my life to protect
this perfect raging strength,
because she's not only the thunder
she's also the lightening
   she's the whole goddamn storm
     she's that moment of quiet
       before dynamite fires."

HELIUM HEART

I learned to look for his face, sharp in the small sunlight of the early morning when we ran together.

All I wanted
was for him to see me,
take my hand,
hold me close,
and take me home.

In the midst of all the pain,
I see a light, finally
and not the light of bridges burning
below me
but the cool light of the moon
as I turn my eyes to the stars
I blow away the smoke
that had clouded them for so long.

CARLIN PIERCE

I didn't realize until I broke my legs, how much, just how much, I was running from monsters I was sure pursued me.

When the light comes
let me wake up next to you
    let's take our swords
        battle the demons
    slash the screams
rend the dark so light may shine again
    and if we die
        let it not be by demon hands
            let it be in each other's arms
                as the cold glow of the stars, far
    away,
fades for the warmth of dawn
let us see the sun again.

HELIUM HEART

If you learn me
just to conquer me,
your siege will
be far
from
bloodless.

CARLIN PIERCE

What did he run from? That wasn't what propelled him; it's not what drives him forward now.

Sweet boy,
    you know nothing
        of the man you will become.
   Be gentle, on your way there,
the uncharted path to a peak
   is not known for easy footing,
      and I know you'll stop
        for nothing.

HELIUM HEART

One day he will wake up and realize that he is all alone,
    because the people who sacrificed everything
    for him had nothing left to give,
    and he had not budged an inch for them.
    He will then perhaps
    realize that bridges collapse
    more often than they
    catch fire.

CARLIN PIERCE

Something pulls at him; he has some strange touch of fate, blessed maybe, and what he saw was in front of him, never over his shoulder.

He was kind and tame,
until he decided to set
   the world on fire,
      then he opened the doors
   to his heart
and let loose his love
beautiful and terrible.

HELIUM HEART

People leave.
That's what they do,
like feathers shed
or snakeskin
we cannot hold tight
to that which is desperate
to become
dust.

CARLIN PIERCE

I loved that about him, as much as I wanted to shake him at the same time "this is not real!" I wanted to scream, "Why don't you know pain?"

Someday you'll miss me
   you'll miss the here and now
      you forgot to be a part of
         because you were living in the past
           or preparing for the future.
              But I watched you in the now
                 I saw your eyes sweep over me
                 I felt the ice of your touch
                     when it couldn't find me
                         in the time of your mind's life.
                         It couldn't feel me at all,
                             and I couldn't thaw
                     your heart
                      for the present
                         for the spring frosts
                            and summer lush.
                         You missed so much living
                         for
                            today
                            yesterday.
But no matter, no matter,
   I just had to wait for your glacier to recede;
        it wasn't my turn to be loved
      yet.
     I had to wait
        until you couldn't touch me,
           couldn't hold me,
        couldn't see me,
           for you to reach for me
               look for me,
                 love me.
    I wasn't in the right time for you.

HELIUM HEART

I am flesh and flaw
imperfect and present
wild and behind you.
    That's how I know you loved me,
    that's how I know you'll miss me.
Because when you look at her face
  someday, you'll live in my eyes
      long gone.

CARLIN PIERCE

But at the same time, I would die before I let anyone or anything hurt him. Perhaps that's why I still can't walk away.

>Please, my boy, shine through
>   your clouds.
>When you cry, I cry
>   and I haven't built an ark.

HELIUM HEART

        I know you keep your phone
        by your bed when you sleep
        at night
        in case someone needs you.
        I wish you'd never seen
        exactly how much I wish
        I could finally be enough.
        But I know people well enough
        by now to know
        they never change. Not even
        the perfect ones,
        not even the ones to trust.
        They can't help it
        their ego predictable
        when they're whole—
        they're so immune to the pain
        that I'd never wish upon them
        but somehow still expect them
        to understand.
        Perhaps people really can't be good.
Perhaps it's not their fault.

CARLIN PIERCE

Perhaps that's why I won't let the hard ground rush up to meet my diving figure; to recover and to walk away would mean losing him forever, and I don't think he knows how much he could not endure that.

        "I watched her for sometime,
        striking match after match,
        I never said anything, of course—
        she wouldn't have wanted that
        but I still watched her
        lighting herself on fire.

        I did ask her about it once,
        after she'd struck a spark
            why she did it, why she
                fanned herself into flames.
        She looked at me in surprise
        'why, someone's got to keep them warm.'"

HELIUM HEART

I really wish I didn't fall in love.
Love is such a stupid word.
How can a single word take the meaning of such big
        emotions?
Really.
It fucking hurts to fall
"Actually it's only the landing that hurts"
at least that's what the girlfriends say to make the pain
        go away
ah, but the pain never *really* goes away
you just get used to it
not really used to it, but expecting it
it's kind of abusive you know?

it's supposed to feel amazing
it's supposed to be powerful and uplifting
and poetic

fuck poetic
this poem sucks
I wish love didn't.
But alas…
And there's the poetry again.
But whatever. It's fine

This is why we eat M&Ms.
This is why we don't see us as beautiful.
This is why we rant.
This is why we fall in love over and over again.

Because it makes us feel so god damn good
except when it doesn't.

CARLIN PIERCE

I can't let him see how people let you down, and how you love them still. He is too much angel for this. He belongs in the clouds, I am convinced.

        He was the flakes of stars
        that fell not white but light
        that shown upon my face
        and made me feel
more than human.

HELIUM HEART

Do you know exactly
    how many times
    I've been told
    to be patient?
    How many times
    I've been told
    just to wait?
    Because someone, someday,
    will want me?
    Ah, but then, do you know
    how many times, how often
    I'm advised to live in the moment?
    Well, which is it?
    All you, with wisdom,
    stay or wait?
    Dive or practice patience?
    I couldn't tell you
    all I know is it hurts
just the same.

CARLIN PIERCE

Sometimes when I can't keep up, I run behind him and my heart breaks, because I know he won't search for me behind him—he doesn't know how to respect the living past.

        I looked back quietly,
        on the footprints in the snow,
alone.

HELIUM HEART

"She was music
strange and untouchable,
    magic made mundane.
        When you saw how she was played,
    you have to see her
        looking over her shoulder
            disappearing around corners
    a part of her body.
        Her sigh you can hear, there
            though you know she's long gone.
That's her perfection.
Don't try to play her strings,
    touch her hair,
make her more than a ghost
    that haunts the air
like a tune you heard
when you were young
    a melancholy lullaby,
        small whispering of grace
           and finality
               and all those things
                    we know somehow
                        to be true
                            but can never
                  make real."

CARLIN PIERCE

So too often I sprint to keep up with him—not to outstrip him, but to run beside him and maybe, just maybe, draw his gaze just off the path in front of him.

>I should not
>have to beg
>to be visible.
>I am
>   so much more
>than your guardian
>angel.

>If I am asking you to break me
>I expect to be your last
>   I expect beautiful ripping
>   apart of souls
>   because both of ours
>   together
>   were too much
>   for the other to bear.

HELIUM HEART

He's never looked, not for anything more than pity, no matter how much I pretended differently to myself.

Why am I not enough
for you?
You are my everything
for so long
your indifference
has been holding
an empty space
in my heart
and I tried to convince myself
for years
that I would be enough
that someday, I would be your person
the same way that you are mine.
Fools, all, who thought love reciprocated
was any more reality than a fairy tale.
One side will never be enough
and just between us,
you should be so lucky,
to find a girl
who can drag as many burdens as she does
and still take everyone
upon her shoulders.
But, maybe, yes maybe, you don't want
a martyr, maybe you don't want a tigress,
I don't know what you want,
but you can't tell me why
it's not me.
Something about me is just never enough.

CARLIN PIERCE

I think I understood I loved him when he knew what not to say, when
he knew what not to say when I needed him to be quiet.

How now? She cried, why me?
    Because you can take it.
He replied, as he gathered her in his arms,
    so normally distant, so careful with space.
His gesture swept her breath away.

She knew in that moment, she knew in her heart
    he'd never let her world fall apart
again, but he'd never know how much
    this felt like a promise, and
a broken promise so shatters a trust.

And broken words and shattered trust
    were her norm for so long from girlhood
        to teendom, and teendom to grown-up.
    Men did what they wanted, unless she guided
        them—and guide she did,
but with him she never had to place his
   feet on a path, one in front
      of the other,
like others she'd moved in the past.

He was warm, he was structure, and of such
architecture, you'd think he was
    carved by a god.
But his mind and his heart were
    his true treasures—never broken
      he cared.

How now, she whispered into his chest
how now to return to mere mortals of men
I've been comforted, held, I've been saved by a god,
when before only pain and injury my men caused.

HELIUM HEART

He said not a word, he simply kissed her hair,
    squeezed her tighter and smiled sadly standing
    there—
he'd love her forever, he knew that inside.
  He'd told her as much, when she was down on her pride.

But love and in love are not the same thing,
she knew this and he knew that she'd never cling
    to him if he chose to go his own way,
but as far as she'd seen, men fled when they promised to stay.

She wanted him close; he couldn't make her believe
that he'd made up his mind, that he'd never leave
her side, but she couldn't know, standing there in such arms
she'd never known before, she dared not hope,
  for hoping only made the heart sore.

So they stood in silence, how now to speak
when words would so violently
  rip them apart, or so they expected,
but such expectations doomed love to
marble hearts that bound the soul.
    So they stood there, he held her—
tried to mend her rent hole.

CARLIN PIERCE

When finally I succumbed to tears, as I felt the world rip off my shoulders, he blindly placed a hand on it and rolled it back into place.

He asked her
how she chose to carry
the pain inside herself.
"Not why?" she answered,
question with question.
"Ok then, reason"—he couldn't
understand.
I cannot lose you—she looked him
in the eye.
He blinked. "But you hurt for me—
you do, don't like, now that
I'm looking I can read it in your eyes."
Now it was her turn to frown
and look to him, surprised.
"How does that matter?" she shot back,
and he took that to heart.
"I don't ask you for martyrdom—"
"No, you merely ask me to do my part."
And my part in this path, untread,
is to be there for you—
for you and all the lost boys
who struggle like you do."
"But—" he started for all he heard was
"weak,
you're weak and I am here
to support you when you
weep."
She understood, she knew the drill,
for men she'd always be
their guiding light, their
mother, daughter, wall to hit, or angel never free.

"But how?" He'd stopped and looked her in the face—
she couldn't

HELIUM HEART

make him see her heart—
he blind and she unwilling—
"Well I can carry what you can't"
she said this very simply.
"I'm strong!" He said—
as he stuck out his chin.
She smiled sadly, having stopped
and reached up to his cheek.
"You're strong in body, blood, and bone
and stubborn pride, of course...
but," she sighed, "you'll never know
the muscles that only seem to grow,
that burst to life within the heart
when from young age
your life brings trial,
and you of all know all my life
how can you ask how I still stand—
and how I will forevermore—
when you alone know all the scars
that rest upon my soul.
You ask me how I still stand straight
when atlas is my role...
Well you should know that
when you broke my love
I didn't choose to give you,
you should have understood by now
that I am stronger, so much
stronger, than you will
ever know."

CARLIN PIERCE

*He couldn't know at that moment, he was pushing my cracks together,
making my fractures whole again.*

>Maybe one day
>I'll heal fully,
>beautiful
>breaks
>accepted
>within me
>fire from the phoenix
>will meld me back together.

HELIUM HEART

"She wanted to heal people.
Perhaps it was her brother,
    perhaps it was her father's failure,
        perhaps she just had that heart
            you know the type—
        that heart which, if you ever get a glimpse,
            will burn you
                from the inside out.
She wanted to help, to help people grow,
but her heart, it was too strong
    for most souls.
        It was the kind of heart
            that melts lesser men,
                but draws them yet towards its
                    light.
Guarded she'd built walls
around it, she knew not what it had become.
    She only knew what she could feel
        up there, behind her eyes,
            but mirrors, well mirrors don't show
  the tigers eyes—
            they betrayed her heart;
    she did not know
        she could not see
      how hot, how dazzling bright,
        how dangerously
                her heart lit up the world."

CARLIN PIERCE

This backfired. This external balancing. I learned to expect him.

>I have to ask you to leave
>not because I wish to see you go
>>not because I wish to be alone
>but because
>with your presence
>I lean into you
>>(even when I don't mean to)
>and I will break
>when given freely
>>a crutch
>put pressure on my fractures
>press my breaks together hard.
>I must hold myself straight,
>>my burdens on my own shoulder.
>Lessening my pain, dearest,
>will shatter me.

HELIUM HEART

Walk among wolves, dear girl,
so you'll know when you find a sheep;
    don't settle for anything less
    than one who howls at the moon.

CARLIN PIERCE

I learned to lean into him, to love again and to somehow crave in a way I never thought I'd be able to.

My sheets smell like you.
I still sleep with your pillow
   between my legs
wrapped up inside my arms
      like you used to be
      inside me.
But all that's left of you
are feather flashes,
    a small scent of whiskey,
  and sex.
Your toothbrush was pink, I don't know why
it's still next to mine.
   Maybe I'll throw them away together,
  easier to discard domestic bliss
      in one fell swoop
       than to let half linger
         in these scenes implying
           intimacy, lost.
Yes, let's burn it all together.

HELIUM HEART

Oh, my innocence
I don't think
    Band-Aids
will suffice
anymore.

CARLIN PIERCE

Foolish, simple, silly predictable love.

   Are you pure luck?
      Me puddle jumping
 at the right time?
      Or would you have
happened to matter what?
       Were you the ocean?
       Inevitable and
       inescapable.

HELIUM HEART

Pisa probably thought
her love would last
too.

CARLIN PIERCE

Why did I expect him to see me as I saw him? Why did I expect to be the exception?

    She was the long-term, wife-type
    they all said they wanted
    when they came to her to ask
    how to handle their women.
        She wasn't shiny, but she shone
          she knew
            she was plain, no sparkle, not dull
              but not new.
    She was the familiar, the mother figure
    the one they'd leave
        on a ship, burning or sinking
          because she
          "could handle it."
    She was the responsible, the caretaker
    the ballerina in a world that
        values strippers and excess
        she could dance by herself
          sans pole, sans man
            she held herself up—
              "Fragile ego, don't be scared."
    She held the world, like Atlas
    but, no Titan, she could not stay
        in the mountains alone
          instead she bore the world in the world
            still incredibly alone.
    She didn't mind, she knew humans
    there were only ten types
        they listed themselves
            as they revealed their souls.
    She wasn't quite like any of the ten,
    she was loyal and brave
        and she knew where to stand, what to say
          how to make men think

HELIUM HEART

    but never could she make them see
        beyond her mask, the sinking ship,
      the world, the mountains,
        the long-term,
          the phoenix.
She was the one, she knew in her heart,
perhaps she was the eleventh person,
    the only one in the dark, like her
    she shed light, around them,
      the lost boys.
          But where she could see in the dark,
      they couldn't see her
and she refused to illuminate herself to the world.

CARLIN PIERCE

Because I am vain and, despite all my pain, all my betrayals, all my crushed expectations, I am still a dreamer.

I want you to tell me
    that I'm your one,
        that despite all the walls
        you've thrown up
        against potential mates,
    that I'm the one who climbed
over mine.
Because, you see my love,
    you are so much more to me
    than words or walls.
By your side,
    I am whole,
    and I want to walk,
    more than anything,
        by your side
    into forever.
Trust in me, my love, I am strong.
I am present and I'm perpetual.
Please open your eyes—
See me, my love, *see me*.
Return my epithet for you—
    you don't have to do this alone,
    believe it or not,
    sometimes people can just be good.
Your heart can learn its missing piece
    is sitting right in mine;
    look inside me, my love,
    look and leap—I'll catch you always.
To this I swore
    to you, my love, I'll give my last
        breath.
Please know, dearest, I'll wait
though patience is not my virtue,
I'll wait for you.

HELIUM HEART

Dark lipstick and white wine.
That was all he remembered of her,
the dimpled stain her lips had left along the rim.
They'd stuck slightly, on the glass
when she'd pulled away.
He shuddered.

She might have well been
a walking fire,
but he hadn't gotten close enough
to touch.

CARLIN PIERCE

And he's my dream. I told his sister-in-law that last weekend, when she told me not to give up.

When I think of you
you ethereal, nebulous person
I hope to spend most of my life with,
when I think of you, future companion,
I think of black coffee that
    scalds the tongue,
and four pieces of cinnamon gum
all at once, *burn* me with your whisper,
of bitter whiskey, that
makes my tongue
    curl, when I smell you,
    and my lips, thirsty.
I think of those balloons you see sometimes,
floating lazily in the sky,
    set free from a child's hand, most likely,
        and you, you're a red balloon in a
            grey-cloud sky,
            a wanderer I can't help but follow.
You're those bookstores, nestled in the
crooks of buildings, where books lead
such chaotic, adventurous lives
    in and out of the hands of gods.
But, future person, you're also the country,
you're the sunset, caught in the
waist of the hill, so brilliant
    and so blindingly beautiful,
        you can't but know you exist
to end a story.
You're meant to be dangerously devastating.

To be brief, because you're so much
you're old newspapers, cold pizza in the morning,
those clouds that somehow make shapes (particularly
dinosaurs), you're the chimneys of old farmhouses, city bricks,

HELIUM HEART

Colorado lightning, black chucks,
beat up soccer balls, black boards over whiteboards,
black and mild's on locked balconies,
ivy covered fences, long kisses, hard walls,
red wine snuck out of a backpack, planes
landing right over your head as you scream
and no one can hear, you're climbing trees in the dark,
sharp stars and soft wishes, you're that certain color green
that makes me smile but I don't know why because
my favorite color is purple, you're hardwood mahogany tables,
reading glasses left on the counter in the morning,
pencil shavings and typewriters, old t-shirts and no pants,
that breeze on the top of the mountain when every leaf
shakes in the sun, you're sawdust, you're daffodils out of
snow, you're an open window on summer nights, smooth
diving into rivers, that first gasping of breath after going
too deep, you're November rain, July bonfires,
sea glass and sharks teeth, you're cinderblock buildings
with mad-good graffiti, slow motion glass shattering
and beat-up baseball caps,
you are all the things I find beautiful
in this cracked world.

Come touch the glass, and help me see reality
without a window pane
so here's to you, future companion, be ready for me.

CARLIN PIERCE

So tell me my love,
where is our
    next mountain?

HELIUM HEART

But how can I not I give up on him sometimes I wonder? How can I not willfully wrench my heart from his grasp?

I don't know how to
   put my craving for you
      into words.
You heat me
   from the inside
      out
and I simply cannot
   fight fire with fire
if I want to survive.
   But lately…
      Well perhaps burning would
   not be the worst thing
   is it arson of my soul
      if I beg you for the match?
      No, burn me down in an inferno
      that even the stars would
            envy.

CARLIN PIERCE

Beat, my heart
like a drum
apparently
my blood
burns only
for your indifferent hands.

ah, my love
    please take my tears
they're all I have left
    to give

HELIUM HEART

I know he'll never love me like I love him. I know this too well, no matter how is actions would say differently sometimes. No matter how much I want him.

I still don't think he understands
just what it means when I say
I cannot see another's face
I wish he could feel my pain—
just for a moment, of course—
someone who can feel like I do
should come with a warning
on the side of her box
"Damaged Goods"
maybe then people would stop playing
with something so fragile
maybe he wouldn't have
picked me up
the way he did
maybe he would have watched me
from afar.
I don't know which is better now—
knowing the pain of being played
with and ripped apart—
if perhaps it would have been
better
not to have been desired
from the beginning
rather than to be left again,
unwanted,
tested, torn, tortured in the end
and still not quite enough
I can't even get back in the box
now
there's not enough of me left.

CARLIN PIERCE

I almost wish
you'd try to replace me
plagiarize me
for copies are just never
as good
as their original.

You should have appreciated
what you had
for I am priceless,
timeless,
haunting.

HELIUM HEART

Sometimes I picture us in the future. We have our own house; he's playing catch with our son, sandy hair with green eyes and his smile already wrinkles the corners of his eyes. His father's eyes are long since friends with the crow's feet that tell gently of our laughter. Our daughter is on my hip, as I make sure nothing is burning on the grill. His brothers are due soon, and my brother is already here, making a salad in the kitchen. Our toddler bounces happily on the back porch; his grandmother is watching him. Our garden is in full bloom, tomatoes are so red on their vine, and our dogs are asleep in the shade. I catch his eye for a moment, as he spins our son around, still holding the football and laughing hysterically. I have everything I've ever wanted, and when he mouths "I love you" I know he does too.

CARLIN PIERCE

Take me home
    hold me in your arms
        like clean laundry, warm
    let's hide under it on our sheets
        under the covers
            face to face.

    Kiss me
quietly now, don't wake the baby
    time passes even in dreams
where white picket fences
    loom out of the darkness
        and paint samples
            baby blue or pink?
Guess,
    what I want—it's easy.
        It should be—can't you see my tears?
Please don't leave,
    we have so much more to make,
    please.
I have too much of your home in me
    it will scar
        if you burn down your house.
Arsonist.
    Take me home instead, please
        or give me my dreammaker back.
           Don't blow down my heart
Wolf.
        You'll find more than picket fences
        or pigs there.
    And I've never wanted to hurt you.

HELIUM HEART

Pour me out like your sweet tea
I too have been on your back porch
    face to the sun.
Put me to your lips and taste me
slowly.

CARLIN PIERCE

Surprise. I'm back and the pen is in my hand and my whole future fantasy is popped and has fallen back to simple scratches on a legal pad.

> How can I still hope for him
> when I know he will never love me
> like I love him
> how can I still hope for him
> like I've never hoped before
> when I'm empty for him
> stone and fury out and in
> doomed to darkness, laughing bitter
> to the end.

HELIUM HEART

How can she pick up her pen
and write again
about him?
well, dearest, that's the only way she knows
to lick her wounds
and slowly
start to
heal.

CARLIN PIERCE

Is this as close as I'll ever get to love? Probably. At some point I need to be honest with myself.

>She knew pain so well
>she sometimes wondered
>>if she invited him in
>>>or if she liked his sensation
>>>in her heart.
>>No, she rationalized,
>>>she didn't like him
>>>but the relief
>>>when he left
>>>when joy pierced pain
>>>>was glorious, was rapture
>>>was reason to let the pain
>>>back in, again.

HELIUM HEART

Years later, he'd remember her eyes.
He did, he saw them flash
    in every woman that came after her
every time he met her eyes
he pushed the door to her soul
    a bit further open.
And there's something about the
insatiable thirst to prove oneself
that drives little boys
    to play with fire
        to poke tigers,
   but within those almond eyes
    behind that opened door
        lay fire that burned
          his innocence to ash
          and an amazon's pet
        who clawed his heart
          to pieces.
She'd warned him, amber eyes aglow,
not to tempt a tigress.
    She'd break the boy.
    She'd build a man.
       And he'd be scarred
          forever.

CARLIN PIERCE

That's how I'll finally figure out how to hit the ground, or so my friends say at least. How would I know?

If we could choose
for whom we fall
I wonder if I'd still pick you
because I didn't need
a crystal ball
to know how we'd end
like this—
we'd end in pieces
dust and stone.
Marble doesn't know
how to break
clean.

HELIUM HEART

I find myself spending
    much of my time
these days
    waiting in airports
bound for a predestined
    destination.
But while my body moves
    from place to place
    with intention
    my heart is still
    wandering aimlessly
    with you.
My mind split half
    in the plane
half in your kitchen
    chastising my heart
if only it had rekindled
    its passport, maybe
maybe I could
    move on.

CARLIN PIERCE

I still refuse to give up hope.

To write about healing
is to believe it exists.
There is no reparation
to a shattered soul.
There is only melting down
and remolding, in attempts
to find a shape and shield
to protect from future
falls.

HELIUM HEART

Don't worry, I tell the little voices in my head
  to shut up all the time; emotional
  self-preservation is unnecessary.

>He fit her pattern
>perfectly
>cocky, beautiful, naive.
>And yet, she still dreamed
>of picket fences
>of shadows only
>under trees
>and out of her heart
>of the self-made stitches
>in her chest
>finally healing.
>
>But her dreams and her patterns
>were not the most compatible.

CARLIN PIERCE

Would you take my heart
    in payment for your soul?
My love for your body?
My silence for your thoughts?
Give me your wholeness
let me ravage it
    break your innocence
show you color
    and ecstasy.
I promise to return your pieces
used, of course,
    but I cannot promise
they will be ready
    for any other customer.
Sorry.
Feel free to charge me more.

HELIUM HEART

I'd rather feel full of pain than empty of everything... right?

    Sometimes she felt like a clown.
    Not because she had the power
    to make people laugh,
    but because she found
    the only way
    she could show people
    she was sad
    was when she painted a tear
on her cheek.

CARLIN PIERCE

We used the first half of the night
   for words and raised voices
     and the second half
         for hard kisses and shallow breaths.
The words stung like light scratches
   and throbbed, bruises to the heart;
      hands up, fists closed, left hook-
        practice, they say, makes perfect.
      We only cry inside over invisible wounds.
We know the pattern, the tells
   when to duck and cover,
     come back with a strong
       word to the jugular
         from the tongue.
            Too easy—he didn't block;
        he's quiet.
And in the silence that falls, always
   in the moments when the last echo
     settles—you know the quiet—
       we tumble together—hard.
        Our lips light fire in the night,
           our hands hold the other's soul,
           gently, gently now,
              don't crush it
        We breathe together.
So alive it hurts, so broken by hammer
   strikes to the heart,
     the body flails
       as the execution continues
         deep, deep into the night.
With the morning comes dark looks
   and resignation, but smooth
     holdings of sharp words;
       too long a pattern created.
Peace is not what fighters know.

HELIUM HEART

Right. He reassures me of this somehow, even as my heart attempts to hold its scar tissue body together with electrical tape.

He told me that
sometimes people can just be good.
He lied. But he didn't know it.
He thought he could paint my
lenses with a rose
how beautifully naive
he was.
I pray he never
learns how to see
below their smiles
or read their eyes.

CARLIN PIERCE

I'm finally shattered far and wide
enough
that I no longer wish to pick up
the pieces
because it takes too long—
much too long—
to put them back together
just to break again.

HELIUM HEART

*I've run out of duct tape, and anyway, maybe electrical tape
will conduct your lightning better; nothing else has worked.*

>I think I have finally
>learned my lesson.
>
>There is only so much pain
>a person can take.
>
>And the ones who hurt the deepest
>are the ones you never really
>thought that would.
>
>I think it's time to say goodbye
>for hope is much too fickle,
>and if to live and breathe again,
>
>I cannot hope for love—
>I cannot risk my heart for hope
>for she is not a course of action.
>
>And I would like to have something
>something small of me
>left for me in the end.
>
>Perhaps that is my problem.

CARLIN PIERCE

I stopped and smelled a rose
    once.
That one you gave to me
    deep red are roses
    your eyes were blue
        I wish now I could forget
        this stupid rose
        but mostly I wished I'd
    never stopped
    for you.

HELIUM HEART

I often get mad at you. Livid. I want my freedom back.

To you,
I need to write you a letter. Perhaps a poem in a letter,
I need you to know,
Things   yes things I cannot seem
    to say… out loud.
I love you, I love you to the moon
and back with the depths
    of the roots of the mountains.
Believe me when I say
    I don't want anyone *else*…
But you may not want anyone.
    Be my neighbor then, please?
I don't think
               I can live with out you
    I don't think
I'm sorry. I wish I could be empty.
But to know now what would be
    leaving my heart
if I became hollow
    is not worth losing
        not for anything.
You're my person. You are part of my life
In a way that has taken my soul.
    Fuck you.
I hate you for becoming my gravity.
I gave you my freedom
Which I fought for my whole life,
    and you didn't even ask for it,
        you don't even want it,
    so how can I ask for it back
when you don't know you possess it?
For that matter, while I'm asking for my freedom
why don't you give me my heart back
    gently—it tore when I gave it to you
    ripping it out of my own chest

> holding it out to you on a silver
> > platter, that you didn't see
> > > so long I held it up for you
> > > > that my arms failed me.

But somehow, you still ended up
the proud owner
> of a bruised and beating heart.

You don't even know
I'd sooner die than part from you,
> even if I cannot hold your heart
> > the way you have mine.

To be with you is to breathe
easy and necessary,
> don't suffocate me.
> > Please.

Don't leave me.
Because I don't change. I *am* the mountain,
please don't be my sunset—
alighted on me only for a few moments,
each night, as you disappear
where I can't follow.
I need you to know there is no one else
and even if I find another bedmate,
fondness is not the same thing as wrenching, wretched love.
> Fuck you.

Give it back—you've stolen all of me,
and I would go with you anywhere you asked.
I don't want to.
> Powerless is not the woman
> > I made myself to me.

Then you.
Then you came along.
> And I thought you'd be a nice chapter
to flip back to, fondly,
> fondness is easy.

But I realized too late

HELIUM HEART

    too far into the story,
that your chapter was actually
    the whole story.
Please don't make me Juliette
or Titania.
    Please.
I already hate that I love you so much.
I'm going to shatter.
    That much I know—
I've too many cracks,
    and too much pressure
    (and too much hot air inside)
will you be there
    to piece me back together?
Or will you make me your mosaic?
Beautiful, broken, on your wall
    with only your eyes
        indifferent
    upon me?
Love, me

CARLIN PIERCE

I want that hot flood out of my gut when you surprise me by being here when I don't expect it.

Somehow, when his lips
brushed her skin,
the stars, so far away
burst into flame
for the heat in her
heart
was too great
for the earth to bear.

There are few feelings
as incapacitating
as the shame for love
in my gut
that sits down
hot
hot
hot
until I'm cold.

HELIUM HEART

I don't want to rely on him. But I think I already do.
I've never relied on anyone before. I let people lean on me.

Believe in me
dear gods,
please believe in me.
I don't know how to make
you know
I'll never let you down.

The beauty she possessed
and her broken baggage in hand
did not endear them to her
if anything
she made them feel weak
they had not walked through fire,
they did not live with
all they had.

CARLIN PIERCE

Everyone needs to lean on someone sometime, but I fancy myself superwoman. A martyr of sorts; give me your problems like the world gives Lady Liberty her tired, her poor. I promise I'll hold you all up.

"She's as smooth and steady
as the sea
    when it's pleased.
She doesn't need a partner,
but if you wish to walk
    by her side
into forever
    you must learn
to be the sky
    see your reflection
        in her eyes
    but you must accept
        that you'll only brush her
    on the horizon
but do know that for your patience
she'll reward you
    if she finds you worthy
        with a love as deep
            as the ocean itself."

HELIUM HEART

She is not your
    painting
to regard from afar
    critique without
    knowing her
    making.
She's more than
    her brushstrokes,
more than mere
    memory.
If she hangs herself
    for you
take note.

CARLIN PIERCE

*But I am a hypocrite, I cannot hold myself up now without him,
anymore than Ms. Liberty can bend to place a giant arm
around the huddled masses seeking refuge.*

Do you think life is precious?
Would you pick up the blossom
    that fell from the cherry tree
        still pink?
What if it was a leaf,
brown and crumbled
    that an oak tree dropped
        before you?
When you kiss your grandfather,
who you have outgrown
    do you cry when you see his eyes—
        so much life lived trapped in
    a dying body
what do you do to free a living memory?
How do you give your child the world
    to set on fire?
We raise failed arsonists
    and praise them for sparks.
Have we a fear of fire?
    We'd be foolish not to.
        Death, we know not intimately
but life, life we make our mistress,
use and abuse her,
and take her for granted.
    Why don't we marry her?
Mark her as precious?
    Because we are cowards,
blind and willful.

HELIUM HEART

You know why she's not married, Ms. Liberty?
Not because she chooses to maintain her independence
from a lover, from a love, but because her love
will never love her back like she needs.

> How to start a small piece
> to put words from my mind
> that wrest me from sleep
> please know that I tried.

> I ask here and now
> why I'm never enough
> to what end and how
> might I be seen as above?

> A thought always second
> to those that I love
> I come when I'm beckoned
> then to the side I am shoved.

> I see all the thoughts
> that play through their minds
> and myself not a loss
> when my face they can't find.

> Beautiful I am not
> of that I'm aware
> but you think they'd o'er look that
> for my brain or my care…

> I am not the woman
> the woman they want
> I play too the man
> with nothing to flaunt.

> They want not the tattoos
> or the rings in my ear—

85

CARLIN PIERCE

they want not the taboos
or the history I bear.

Perhaps I am stained
considered exhausted
no worth here remains
so proceed with caution.

The dog that arises
when beaten down thrice
who heeds no chastisement
is regarded as ice.

And ice only melts
when heat is applied
yet when need is not felt
no one bothers to try.

So the ice queen remains
falls perpetually short
careful words seem to paint
all perceptions of her.

My mask yet unbroken
save to those special few
who have heard three words spoken
much too far, I love you.

They whom I love
know much of my soul
for that all above
is what I divulge.
To open my flank
for an entrance of love
yet their hearts remain blank
I am never enough.

HELIUM HEART

Bite your tongue girl
    swallow your words.
Let them run around in your veins
    until they are
    what sustains you.
    Until your heart beats these words
    and you know the pain
    of losing your voice
    is not worth crushing his pride.

CARLIN PIERCE

But she'll never let him see her fall, she'll never let him see her drop her torch or shed a tear. Sound familiar? It should but it doesn't, does it?

>All the poems I write for you
>and your broken heart
>somehow came to bare my soul
>when I realized
>falling so hard for you
>would splatter me open
>on the pavement.
>Perhaps I should have drowned
>instead—
>you'd taken my air anyway.

HELIUM HEART

It's so easy to say
    I wish
I wonder.
    Dear girl,
what story you might have lived
    with words you've bestowed upon
    the stars.

CARLIN PIERCE

I've let him in too far; he's seen my torch drop, he's seen my head drop,
my knees fall as I crumble.

        I scared him away—
        too much I loved him
        and he could not understand
        how I cannot love halfway
        how I cannot give half
        of myself to he for
        whom I have fallen
   into fire.

HELIUM HEART

How is it
that by the time
I trust you
you've found another
and I'm left waiting on the
corner.
Somehow it's raining
and I'm watching you drink
coffee together
behind glass.
I want to shatter you now.

CARLIN PIERCE

You know the worst part though, the worst part about this stupid unreturned love? He helps me up when I fall because he does care.

Ask her sometime
   before you ask her for forever
      about the horrors in her heart.
Ask her if she'll crack her ribs for you,
   pry them open gently, their hinges are rusty,
      they're hardly ever used.
Ask her if you can hold it for a moment
   tell her that weight upon her shoulders,
      tell her you can take it for a moment.
         She'll tell you it's carrying that weight
            for this long, that's made her strong.
You know that—tell her so.
   Make sure you still her trembling,
      before you reach for her heart.
         Slowly, don't frighten her.
            Stroke it first, to make sure
         it knows you mean it no harm.
            Don't worry, her ribs won't close around
               your hand—she knows
                  trapping you in there
                     would hurt her more than you.
You're going to notice something now
   that thing you're holding,
        it's not shaped like a heart
           I know you've never held life so close
              but you're still going to recognize
                that it's odd.
             That's the scar tissue.
            That hole there is from his burn a few years ago.
      Those bruises are from you, a few weeks past.
     That big tear, there, that's her father's doing.
   But it still beats.
      Hard.

HELIUM HEART

      She's just grown hard, rigid, walled.
      And guarded.
She'd be a masochist not to.
   So as you watch her face relax, because
   for the first time, she's recognizing that her wings are free,
     know what you are asking of her.
   If you give her heart back and ask
     her to keep her chest open
        you're asking her to be a masochist.
   If you hold it, you give her
     wings, but you keep her grounded;
         she cannot fly without her heart.
   So what will you do?
What can you do with a grounded angel?

CARLIN PIERCE

I wish he would hate me. I wish he would leave me to pick up my stupid pieces. Let me finally close this chapter.

How did we become the way we were?
How did we share lives without reciprocation?
How did we grow roses together
  and fail to notice the thorns
   the thorns that when the petals fell,
     remained.
  And those were the memories that stayed.
     Blood drawn binds, but fingers pricked heal—
the hurt comes from never being able to touch—
from cutting the beauty to hold it
without fear of accidental pain.
That's how we became the way we were.
We didn't embrace the thorns we grew together;
   instead we sliced our perfect moments
   in our desperation to make them last.
But dry petals are so morbid next to dry blood on a dry page
   "May 2017"
as if any date written could make us remember
   the soft and sharp
   of petals and pricks and peace of that moment.
Tempus fugit and thorns grow faster, thicker, longer than petals ever will.
   We couldn't make our peace with that.
   We couldn't find in our thorns
     what we cherish in the velvet red of our roses.
And that is how we became what we were.
   Tired of trying to outrun time.
   Tired of dying our thumbs green.
   Tired of Band-Aids.

HELIUM HEART

I'm ready to hit the fucking ground at moments like this.
I'm mad at myself for stepping off that cliff
so unwillingly and for not taking
greater measures to guard my heart.

> This perpetual discomfort
> that never seems to ebb,
> I think that must be you
> fighting, a gladiator
>   against my heart.
>   If I were any kind of smart,
> I'd give you a thumbs down.

Sometimes I wish I could turn our last page
and see "the end" written in fancy letters.
    There's something so safe
        in those two words.
            They mean no more pain,
        no more uncertainty,
            such security.
We'd have a happy ending of course—
    sail off into the west
    or ride off into the sunset
        at ease with each other, happy—
    you know, the things we can't
            promise in more pages, in life.
Sometimes I think that "the end" would be
incredibly sad, though.
     No more tears, and no more worries,
   but no more battles to win side by side.
    No more peaks to mount together
      frozen in a perfect moment
        seems like a wish fulfilled,
            but you and I are not good
        at standing still.
            You and I, if we are to end,
        should end in fire and water
        the way we lived
        with everything we've got
            and everything around us.
But if we're not to end with a bang
it would be too easy to end with a sunset
        on a page, stagnant.
            I can't put a number on our story.
   That would be too simple, anticlimactic really,
        for characters like us.

HELIUM HEART

It is so easy to fall in love, so hard to fall out of it.

Someday a woman will ask you
    about this book.
        She'll come up and notice
            the poem—think you sensitive and
                charming.
            She'll be right of course.
And you'll tell her
    it was a gift from a girl—
        she's far away now—
           she was a bit odd
                in her way.
            She could see through people
        like ghosts.
And your eyes will glaze over
    as you remember me,
        and the woman will look at you
            sadly,
        because she knows—
    as all women do—
the look of a man
    who no longer carries
        his own heart.
For you too
    became a ghost
      under my gaze.

CARLIN PIERCE

Seasons come and go
   but, my love
summer is dangerous for me
   I melt.
And perhaps, I live for fall
   in my heart.
      Because there is a sweet, if bitter
        certainty
in the inevitable ending of things
   and in the coming winter
  heart, ice cold.

HELIUM HEART

Somehow I loved him more and more as he unknowingly hurt me.

>You of all people,
>my love,
>did not have the right
>to shatter me.

CARLIN PIERCE

Trussed up with
    ropes of screams
I cannot ask for
    release—I know
    you can tie knots
    because I taught you how.
I helped you bind me
    with chains,
    control me,
gave you
    my insides,
    to stretch,
    for yourself—
my inquisition
    for a crime
    I did not commit.
You cannot punish me
    for never loving you.

HELIUM HEART

When he chooses another, when he looks at me like I matter,
like I matter more than anything or anyone,
I want to scream at him yet again;
"how could you find happiness with her? How dare you?"

        I can't breathe
        for the expectation met
        was so much more painful
        than it should have been
        when with every beat my heart
        took as it raced to this conclusion
        it seemed it knew it was running
        towards its end.
        I should have cut it out myself
        instead of heard your words.
        It probably would have hurt less.

CARLIN PIERCE

I'm lying here
in my bed, that you
so recently left
without telling me.
Your heart was already
taken—how was I
supposed to know
the only reason
my heart stuck in your chest
was that yours was a vacuum
because yours was long gone.
To think I had a chance
was to think my sheets
would always smell
like you—
beautiful. And foolish.

HELIUM HEART

When of course all I want for him is joy.
I just want him to see how much I am for him.

> She wished, somehow, that he
> could hear her heart
>   as more than a beat
> for it was crying his name
>   "see me, *see me*"
> "build with me two homes in the mountains
> I want what you want"
> But her heart didn't speak his language
> and language was not her forte.
>   No, she might have been adept at biology,
> but this rebellious, howling heart
> chose poetry, chose a life
>   of misread thoughts.
>   Fool.

CARLIN PIERCE

You know if you crush her
    she smells like roses,
but she lingers,
    haunting.

I used to be jealous
of her,
but then I realized
she would never
sleep in your heart
like I do.

HELIUM HEART

I want him to know how simply I want to be with him
and how raw the rip is every time I leave his presence,
because I know I think about him
a hundred thousand times more than he thinks of me.

                    I've decided that people just can't help
                    being what they are—
                    they're selfish and they fall
                    much too easily.
                    They promise, they pray, they cry
                    and at the end of the day
                    the one thing they cannot do
                    is keep up the charade
                    for themselves or for anyone
                    that anything really matters
                    that anything matters at all.

CARLIN PIERCE

If I put the bottle down
    odds are if it's more
        than half empty
    then I'm with you.
I have to numb myself
to stay safe
from the pain.

HELIUM HEART

And he has every right to bestow his heart upon whom he wishes.
Of course he does. It just makes me want to kill both of them.

>I don't have any words left.
>I gave my heart away
>too many times
>and now,
>well now, I wait.
>Perhaps I'll die for glory
>if I cannot die for love.

She didn't know why he held her at arm's length,
she watched the two of them
so utterly in synchronization, so utterly on different pages,
she'd fallen for fate, for his middle name.
    He'd used her as a crutch, but glorified her
        all the same.
She bent, in child's pose so he might reach
the moon,
    but she, he couldn't see
        was a star- she shone from ages past- small and strong,
eclipsed by the moon, that waxed and waned
at whim.
And he, he tried to claim the moon,
and she, she held his telescope on her shoulder
    until her arms fell from muscle failure.
        He didn't notice
            her, under his feet, behind his eyes
                and on his heart.
She, the other one, watched this dance of
desertion and mislove, she cried
    inside,
        for the star, so full of light,
            warm, but so far from him,
would never cry for herself.

HELIUM HEART

I didn't say I could feel rationally; I only said I could think rationally.

        He was falling deeper
        when there was no deeper to go.

        He was spinning silk
        from milk and honey
        and the gold that only
        sunsets glow.

        He just was, and that—
        well, that and hope—
        were the things
        I never thought that would—
        but broke me
    in the end.

CARLIN PIERCE

But since I had his body... I can't separate heart from mind
from gut—and they all say to run.

> For all the men who have swung a hammer
> at my glass soul, I've been able
> to putty up the cracks.
> If *you* swing, you will shatter me
> more wholly than you can imagine,
> and I truly don't have
> enough horses or men, let alone
> another king, to put me back together
> again.

HELIUM HEART

Red nails and red lips
    dark lashes and dark eyes;
she was everything you've been
    told to run from,
    sweet boy
But you leaned forward
    to play with
    the flames
    anyway.

CARLIN PIERCE

But I can't, I haven't hit the ground yet; I haven't learned to heal yet. Perhaps I'll never find out if it's an ocean.

> Don't make me bow,
> you'll lose me to the stars
>   and the pine trees
>   on the heights
>   you took me to
>   on our first night.
> Don't have me whisper
> my heart will scream
>   and I'll dance on feathers
>   of forgotten birds
>   who never lost their voice.
> But please, oh please,
> don't make me cry
>   we'll both drown
>   as we howl under tears
>   where no one can hear
>   hearts break.

HELIUM HEART

I watched two umbrellas dance
yesterday in the rain
one was red, the other blue
so primary
like colors, like school
so simple, this human act
of getting around each other
so lonely, so together.
I could have giggled, but the rain
made me look like my cheeks
were wet with tears—
I didn't have an umbrella—
And,
not wanting the dancers
to think their audience mad,
I didn't laugh with the sky's tears.
I simply watched them
pirouette out of each other's way,
without so much as a backwards glance.
And just like that
the show was over
the rain had stayed
and I found myself wishing
for a partner
to dance with in the rain.

CARLIN PIERCE

Perhaps my heart will fill with helium instead and I will float up and up and up past Ms. Liberty's torch, past the clouds in which I store my daydreams and in which I am convinced he lives,

> So often I read romance
> into words outside of pages
> probably because I seek stories
> and when asked "after all this time"
>   he says "always"
> I think of you, because you will always
>   be the one I'll give anything for.
>   I've scarred my heart
>   like lightning, over and over
>   (that's not supposed to happen)
> and it doesn't make me a superhero.
>   I suppose if anything,
>   It makes me a survivor.

HELIUM HEART

One day, my to do list
won't have
    "Fix him"
at the top—
one day, I'll realize
how flawless
    your seams are.

CARLIN PIERCE

up and up and up my helium heart until I can see the whole world in front of me, instead of feeling it on my shoulders,

                Love, for her, was an acquired taste.
                It had to be.
                She'd bit too hard into it before.
                It burned her tongue,
                      it scorched her lips,
                      she choked on it.
                She'd quit, cold turkey, for so long
                that now she could only remember
                    the pain
                        and none of the flavor.
                She had to relearn
                how to appreciate the taste
                    of seasoned words
                        and stirring action
                            of the mix of bitter and sweet.
            But in her recovery, she'd learned patience—
              she'd learned how to craft
                  a meal
                      rather than steal a bite.

HELIUM HEART

Don't pretend you're able
to carry the burdens
I carry.
The muscles of my soul
have held such weight that you will
never know
and for that, dearest, though not your
fault—don't think me weak
when I choose to care
and give a second chance
for I am so much stronger
than you will ever be.

up and up and up until I can see the stars fully and thickly without the gentleness they lend to their pinholes-in-blanket perceptions back on earth.

>Perhaps he was the weak one—
>unable to carry all of what
>I am—all of my enoughness.
>
>Perhaps the reason he walked away
>was because when he dropped me
>I did not break
>and there was nothing left
>for him to put back together
>again.

HELIUM HEART

There are flames that candles claim
and there are wildfires.
    She was somewhere in the middle
        gently ravaging
            but relentless.

CARLIN PIERCE

Perhaps I'll make friends with the moon; I'm not afraid of his dark side.

I built myself with bricks
so men like you
could never knock me down,
blow me over.

HELIUM HEART

She was a dandelion
    she bloomed, not for him, not for
anyone.
Wild and bright,
    and when she was ready
she threw herself to the wind
    and spread herself
      for her own enjoyment.

CARLIN PIERCE

Perhaps I'll shatter with all my freedom.

    Dance among the stars,
    dear girl
       the dark
          can't touch you there.

HELIUM HEART

There aren't enough things
in the world
to which one could compare her
because she was too magic
    too mad
        for them, mere mortals
            mere men
    she belonged in wonderland
and they could never follow her.

CARLIN PIERCE

In all my infinite space I am a wanderer, born to fly, not to fall.

If only I had the authority
  to speak on love
  but I know only rocky wisdom
  of pain and repetition
  of dreams and push and pull.
  I'm good at losing hearts
  and if it's knowledge
  on how to win a soul or war,
  I'm not the teacher you should ask
  for I'm still searching
  for myself
  for how to balance
love and loss.

ABOUT THE AUTHOR

Carlin Pierce has published two previous collections of poetry, and now lives in Washington DC. She is a student of language and will receive her BA in Arabic and Theology from Georgetown University in May 2018. "Stopping by Woods on a Snowy Evening" by Robert Frost is still Carlin's favorite poem.

Made in the USA
Middletown, DE
12 August 2019